SEYMOUR PUBLIC LIBRARY
46 CHURCH STREET
SEYMOUR, CT 06483

# REVIVING THE SPIRIT, REFORMING SOCIETY
## Religion in the 1800s

# DAILY LIFE IN AMERICA IN THE 1800s

Bleeding, Blistering, and Purging: Health and Medicine in the 1800s
Buggies, Bicycles, and Iron Horses: Transportation in the 1800s
Cornmeal and Cider: Food and Drink in the 1800s
America at War: Military Conflicts at Home and Abroad in the 1800s
From the Parlor to the Altar: Romance and Marriage in the 1800s
Guardians of the Home: Women's Lives in the 1800s
Home Sweet Home: Around the House in the 1800s
Jump Ropes, Jacks, and Endless Chores: Children's Lives in the 1800s
Reviving the Spirit, Reforming Society: Religion in the 1800s
Outlaws and Lawmen: Crime and Punishment in the 1800s
Passing the Time: Entertainment in the 1800s
Rooting for the Home Team: Sports in the 1800s
Scandals and Glory: Politics in the 1800s
The Sweat of Their Brow: Occupations in the 1800s
Saloons, Shootouts, and Spurs: The Wild West In the 1800s

# REVIVING THE SPIRIT, REFORMING SOCIETY
## Religion in the 1800s

by
Kenneth McIntosh

Mason Crest Publishers

Copyright © 2011 by Mason Crest Publishers. All rights reserved. No part of this publication may be reproduced or transmitted in any form or by any means, electronic or mechanical, including photocopying, recording, taping, or any information storage and retrieval system, without permission from the publisher.

MASON CREST PUBLISHERS INC.
370 Reed Road
Broomall, Pennsylvania 19008
(866)MCP-BOOK (toll free)
www.masoncrest.com

First Printing
9 8 7 6 5 4 3 2 1

Library of Congress Cataloging-in-Publication Data

McIntosh, Kenneth, 1959–
  Reviving the spirit, reforming society : religion in the 1800s / by Kenneth R. McIntosh.
      p. cm. — (Daily life in America in the 1800s)
  Includes bibliographical references and index.
  ISBN 978-1-4222-1783-2 (hardcover)   ISBN (series) 978-1-4222-1774-0
  ISBN 978-1-4222-1856-3 (papercover)   ISBN (pbk series) 978-1-4222-1847-1
  1. United States—Religion—19th century. 2. Religion and social problems—United States—History—19th century. I. Title.

  BL2525.M422 2011
  201'.7097309034—dc22
                                          2010012746

Produced by Harding House Publishing Service, Inc.
www.hardinghousepages.com
Interior Design by MK Bassett-Harvey.
Cover design by Torque Advertising + Design.
Printed in USA by Bang Printing.

# Contents

**Introduction**   6
**Part I: Reviving the Spirit: 1800–1840s**   9
**Part II: Reforming Society: 1840s–1860s**   35
**Part III: The Uneasy Melting Pot: 1860s–1890s**   49
**Think About It**   60
**Words Used in This Book**   61
**Find Out More**   62
**Index**   63
**Picture Credits**   64
**About the Author & the Consultant**   64

# Introduction

History can too often seem a parade of distant figures whose lives have no connection to our own. It need not be this way, for if we explore the history of the games people play, the food they eat, the ways they transport themselves, how they worship and go to war—activities common to all generations—we close the gap between past and present. Since the 1960s, historians have learned vast amounts about daily life in earlier periods. This superb series brings us the fruits of that research, thereby making meaningful the lives of those who have gone before.

The authors' vivid, fascinating descriptions invite young readers to journey into a past that is simultaneously strange and familiar. The 1800s were different, but, because they experienced the beginnings of the same baffling modernity were are still dealing with today, they are also similar. This was the moment when millennia of agrarian existence gave way to a new urban, industrial era. Many of the things we take for granted, such as speed of transportation and communication, bewildered those who were the first to behold the steam train and the telegraph. Young readers will be interested to learn that growing up then was no less confusing and difficult then than it is now, that people were no more in agreement on matters of religion, marriage, and family then than they are now.

We are still working through the problems of modernity, such as environmental degradation, that people in the nineteenth century experienced for the first time. Because they met the challenges with admirable ingenuity, we can learn much from them. They left behind a treasure trove of alternative living arrangements, cultures, entertainments, technologies, even diets that are even more relevant today. Students cannot help but be intrigued, not just by the technological ingenuity of those times, but by the courage of people who forged new frontiers, experimented with ideas and social arrangements. They will be surprised by the degree to which young people were engaged in the great events of the time, and how women joined men in the great adventures of the day.

When history is viewed, as it is here, from the bottom up, it becomes clear just how much modern America owes to the genius of ordinary people, to the labor of slaves and immigrants, to women as well as men, to both young people and adults. Focused on home and family life, books in this series provide insight into how much of history is made within the intimate spaces of private life rather than in the remote precincts of public power. The 1800s were the era of the self-made man and women, but also of the self-made communities. The past offers us a plethora of heroes and heroines together with examples of extraordinary collective action from the Underground Railway to the creation of the American trade union movement. There is scarcely an immigrant or ethic organization in America today that does not trace its origins to the nineteenth century.

This series is exceptionally well illustrated. Students will be fascinated by the images of both rural and urban life; and they will be able to find people their own age in these marvelous depictions of play as well as work. History is best when it engages our imagination, draws us out of our own time into another era, allowing us to return to the present with new perspectives on ourselves. My first engagement with the history of daily life came in sixth grade when my teacher, Mrs. Polster, had us do special projects on the history of the nearby Erie Canal. For the first time, history became real to me. It has remained my passion and my compass ever since.

The value of this series is that it opens up a dialogue with a past that is by no means dead and gone but lives on in every dimension of our daily lives. When history texts focus exclusively on political events, they invariably produce a sense of distance. This series creates the opposite effect by encouraging students to see themselves in the flow of history. In revealing the degree to which people in the past made their own history, students are encouraged to imagine themselves as being history-makers in their own right. The realization that history is not something apart from ourselves, a parade that passes us by, but rather an ongoing pageant in which we are all participants, is both exhilarating and liberating, one that connects our present not just with the past but also to a future we are responsible for shaping.

—*Dr. John Gillis, Rutgers University Professor of History Emeritus*

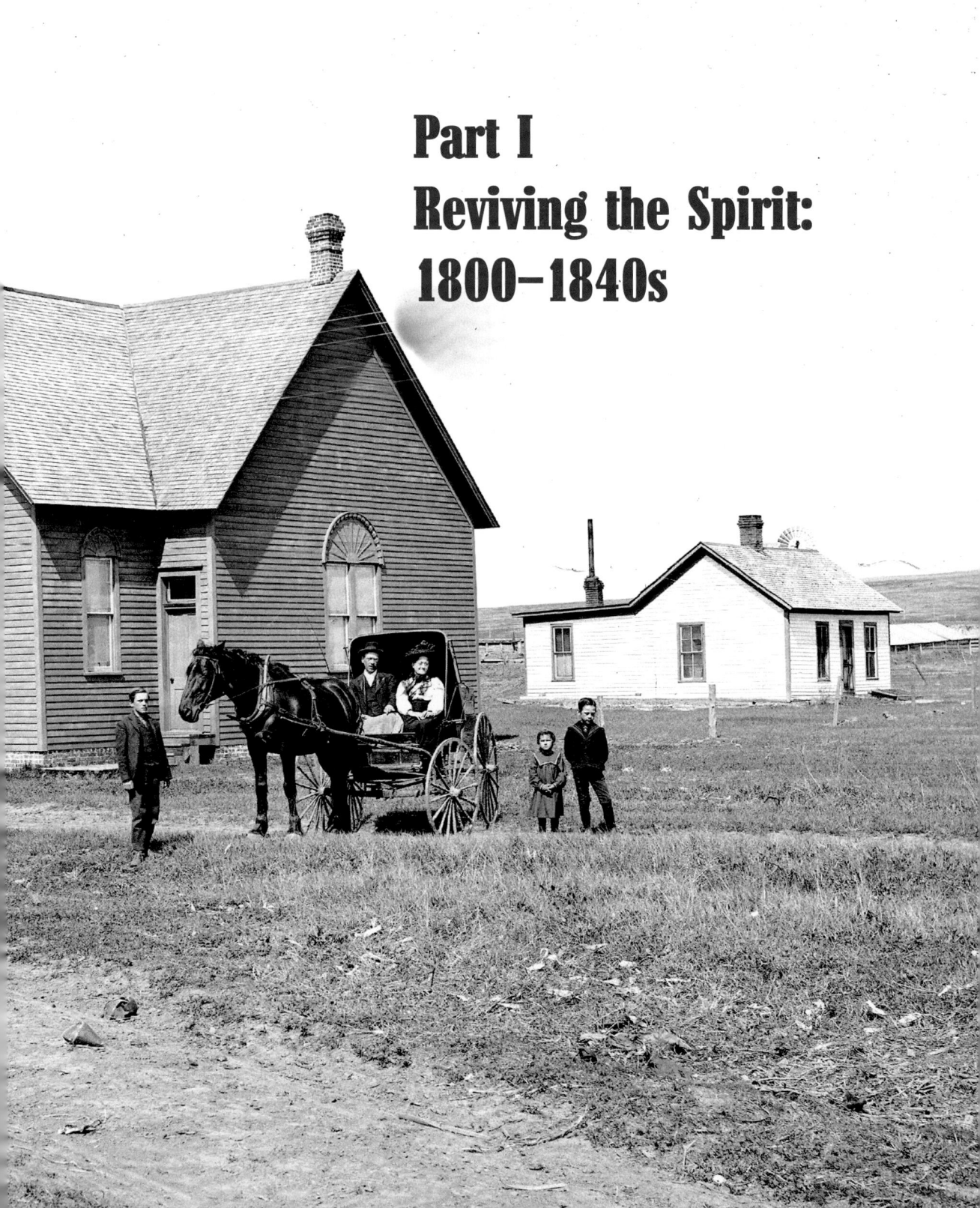

# Part I
# Reviving the Spirit: 1800–1840s

# 1800

1800 The Library of Congress is established.

*1800 The Second Great Awakening begins in the United States.*

# 1801

1801 Thomas Jefferson is elected as the third President of the United States.

# 1803

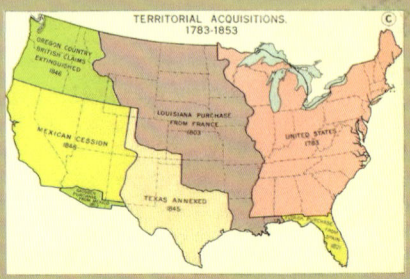

1803 Louisiana Purchase—The United States purchases land from France and begins westward exploration.

*Time Line*

# 1823

1823 Monroe Doctrine—States that any efforts made by Europe to colonize or interfere with land owned by the United States will be viewed as aggression and require military intervention.

# 1825

1825 The Erie Canal is completed—This allows direct transportation between the Great Lakes and the Atlantic Ocean.

*1825 Charles Finney begins preaching and quickly becomes famous.*

# 1830

*1830 Joseph Smith founds the Church of Jesus Christ of Latter Day Saints and the religion of Mormonism.*

## 1804

**1804 Journey of Lewis and Clark**—Lewis and Clark lead a team of explorers westward to the Columbia River in Oregon

## 1812

**1812 War of 1812**—Fought between the United States and the United Kingdom

## 1820

**1820 Missouri Compromise**—Agreement passes between pro-slavery and abolitionist groups. It states that all the Louisiana Purchase territory north of the southern boundary of Missouri (except for Missouri) will be free states, and the territory south of that line will be slave.

## 1833

**1833** Massachusetts becomes the last state in the Union to disestablish state religion.

## 1834

**1834** The Catholic Church officially brings the Tribunal of the Holy Office of the Inquisition, commonly known as the Spanish Inquisition, to an end.

**1834** African American Baptists in Ohio form the Providence Baptist Association, the first group of Black Baptist churches in the United States.

**C**hurch services bored Tom Sawyer. Mark Twain's young hero fidgeted, trying to sit still through long sermons. In one service, Tom amused himself by playing with a "pinch bug." A poodle dog then wandered into the church and began toying with the beetle. When the insect bit, the poodle howled and ran through the church—upsetting the whole congregation. That was Tom's favorite church meeting.

Although Tom Sawyer had little religious interest, he lived at a time when spiritual faith did influence a great number of Americans. In 1831, a Frenchman, Alexis De Tocqueville, visited North America and noted that "the religious atmosphere of the country was the first thing that struck me on arrival in the United

*Part I:* Reviving the Spirit: 1800–1840s   **13**

States." This was the time of revivals, religious gatherings that caused great excitement. Religion dominated the social issues of the day, especially the conflict over slavery. At the same time, Joseph Smith founded a new religious movement—the Latter Day Saints Church, the Mormons.

# Setting the Stage: Religion in Colonial America

Religions in America were already old when the nineteenth century began. For thousands of years, Native Americans had practiced their traditions, and many still follow those same ways today.

Most European settlers were Christians—but that religion came to America already divided. Since 1517, Christianity had split into two hostile camps: Catholics followed the Pope in Rome, while Protestants insisted on each person's right to interpret the Bible privately. In Europe, they fought and killed over these issues.

The English Puritans fled to New England, escaping religious conflict in their homeland, but in the American colonies they continued religious intolerance. Other colonists were Baptists and Quakers—Christians who believed in religious freedom. They influenced

Quakers had no ministers who led their meetings. They believed that the Spirit of God could speak through anyone.

# Bill of Rights

**Congress of the United States,** begun and held at the City of New York, on Wednesday, the fourth of March, one thousand seven hundred and eighty nine.

> Congress shall make no law respecting an establishment of *religion*, or prohibiting the free exercise thereof; or abridging the freedom of *speech*, or of the *press*; or the right of the people peaceably to *assemble*, and to *petition* the government for a redress of grievances.

the United States to promise, "Congress shall make no law respecting an establishment of religion, or prohibiting the free exercise thereof" (the first amendment to the United States Constitution).

# Religious Excitement: The Great Awakening

When the nineteenth century began, many Protestants felt their religion had fallen asleep. Church leaders argued over theology, while people in the churches felt like Tom Sawyer did, bored by irrelevant speeches.

That changed when revivals started; traveling preachers gathered people outdoors for weeklong camp meetings, and thousands attended. These preachers were Evangelicals, Protestants who encouraged emotional conversions. Evangelicals brought religion to the frontier by means of circuit riders—ministers who traveled on horseback, preaching wherever they stopped.

16  *Reviving the Spirit, Reforming Society:* Religion in the 1800s

*Part I:* Reviving the Spirit: 1800–1840s

**Camp meetings were outdoor services, often held under a tent or a structure with only a roof. Sometimes, the roof was built from brush, and sometimes only the speaker had a roof over his head, while the congregation stood under the sun or rain.**

**Circuit riders were ministers who traveled around the countryside on horseback, preaching repentance at services wherever they stopped.**

**Camp meetings were often very emotional, as well as spiritual. The speakers worked the crowd into a frenzy, so that people sobbed, danced, twitched, and fainted.**

The most famous revival meeting was at Cane Ridge, Kentucky. More than ten thousand people gathered in this frontier settlement while Reverend Barton Stone preached enthusiastically. His words had tremendous effect. More than a thousand people reacted intensely; an observer saw people "fall down, cry out, and tremble."

Similar meetings spread throughout the United States. So many people "woke up" spiritually that observers called this "the Second Great Awakening" (another "Great Awakening" had occurred earlier in colonial times). In New York State, there was so much fiery preaching that people called that area "the Burned Over District." Revivals continued for thirty years, springing up throughout America. In 1811,

*Reviving the Spirit, Reforming Society:* Religion in the 1800s

# INCREDIBLE INDIVIDUAL
## Francis Asbury

Frontier settlements were too small to afford pastors for each local community, so the Methodist Church appointed "circuit riders," traveling evangelists—men who spread the Christian faith by preaching in barns, cabins, and fields.

It was a grueling job. Circuit riders worked so hard, that folks had a saying on rainy days: "There is nothing out today but crows and Methodist preachers." Half the circuit riders died before age thirty-three. Those that survived grew tough.

Francis Asbury (1745–1816) was the most famous of this hardy bunch. He was born in England, but came to America as a young man. During his forty-five years of ministry, Asbury traveled more than 300,000 miles on horseback and preached more than 16,000 sermons. He planted Methodist churches in the American frontier, going wherever people were, even in dangerous regions.

Asbury was a school dropout, but he helped start five different schools. He hated slavery and begged his fellow Methodists to end that evil practice. He kept working hard to the very end of his life: after he preached his last sermon, bystanders carried him to his carriage. Hard work and illness had exhausted his body, but by then, thanks to his extraordinary efforts, there were more than 200,000 Methodists in America.

Charles Finney was a celebrity in his day. He used his fame to help bring about the end of slavery in the United States.

one of every five Americans attended a revival meeting, and in 1831, a religious scholar estimated that a hundred thousand Americans had experienced religious conversions—just in that one year!

In 1825, a new celebrity preacher burst upon the scene. Charles Finney insisted that conversion meant more than changing one's beliefs; a converted person must also make the world a better place. This emphasis on reform eventually helped to end slavery.

## Other Religious Voices

In the year 1800, only a small part of North America belonged to the United States: the biggest part of the country belonged to France and Spain. In 1803, with the Louisiana Purchase, and in 1848, with the Mexican-American war, the United States gained the entirety of what are now the lower forty-eight states.

At the time when the United States acquired these western regions, Europeans had already worshipped there, alongside Native peoples, for centuries. Monks from Spain and Mexico worked

Chimayo, New Mexico, has been a center for Hispanic faith since the early 1800s.

The miraculous appearance of a dark-skinned Mary to a Mexican man in the sixteenth century led to the conversion to Catholicism of many Mexican natives. The Virgin of Guadalupe has inspired countless Hispanic Americans ever since.

among Natives and Spanish-speaking ranchers, building adobe mission churches. Hispanic communities developed their own brand of Catholicism, loyal to many saints, rich in fine art, and believing in miracles. In 1810, worshipers at a tiny adobe church in Chimayo, New Mexico, reported miraculous healings. For over two hundred years since then, believers have journeyed to Chimayo for a touch from God—and last year more than 300,000 pilgrims visited that same tiny chapel.

*Part I:* Reviving the Spirit: 1800–1840s

**In the South, white people often felt an obligation to convert blacks to Christianity, even while they enslaved blacks and treated them cruelly. Eventually, however, Christianity was a driving force behind the abolition movement.**

In the early 1800s, the United States promised freedom of religion for some—but not all—people. In the Northern colonies, the Industrial Revolution did away with the need for human bondage—but in the South, slavery increased. Some owners encouraged their slaves to go to church, where sermons emphasized their inferiority. Other owners felt that religion would make slaves "uppity." Of course, Africans had their own spiritual beliefs when they were captured and transported to America—but slave owners regarded tribal religions as "witchcraft" and tried to beat it out of them.

22  *Reviving the Spirit, Reforming Society:* Religion in the 1800s

# EYEWITNESS ACCOUNT

## The Conversion of Jarena Lee

Jarena Lee (1783–1850) grew up to become a famous preacher in the African Methodist Episcopal Church, but she started life as slave to a Philadelphia family. One day the family's cook asked Jarena to come and hear a revival preacher. Jarena describes what happened next:

*My soul was gloriously converted to God under preaching, at the very onset of the sermon. The text was . . . "I perceive thy heart is not right in the sight of God" (Acts 8:21). There appeared to my view, in the center of the heart, one sin, and this was malice—against one particular individual who had strove deeply to injure me, which I resented.*

*At this discovery I said, "Lord, I forgive every creature."*

*That instant it appeared to me as if a garment, which had entirely enveloped my whole person even to my finger's ends, split at the crown of my head and was stripped away from me, passing like a shadow from my sight—when the glory of God seemed to cover me in its stead. That moment, though hundreds were present, I did leap to my feet and declare that God, for Christ's sake, had pardoned the sins of my soul. Great was the ecstasy of my mind, for I felt that not only the sin of malice was pardoned, but all other sins were swept away together.*

From 1845 to 1850, disease wiped out potatoes in Ireland, causing a million deaths from starvation, and sending half a million Irish men, women and children to the United States. Many Irish died in over-packed vessels known as "coffin ships." When Irish immigrants arrived, they faced religious discrimination: they were Catholics, and Protestant Americans did not welcome their faith.

At this same time, settlers increasingly moved into the lands of Native Americans, threatening Native cultures and religions. Most people of these First Nations fought to keep their spirituality.

Handsome Lake was a member of the Six Nations (Haudenosaunee, or Iroquois) who, along with many of his people, suffered from the white men's diseases. In 1799, he received a vision, in which the Creator revealed that his people suffered because they had left their traditional ways. Handsome Lake passed the Creator's words on to others. Many still follow his teaching today.

**During the Irish potato famine, over a million people died of starvation, many of them young children, as portrayed here—and hunger drove a million more to immigrate to the United States.**

24   *Reviving the Spirit, Reforming Society:* Religion in the 1800s

This political cartoon from the 1800s portrays an Irish man and an Irish priest, revealing the racial prejudice that the Irish often faced in the United States.

Many Americans viewed Catholicism with distrust and bigotry, as this political cartoon reveals in its portrayal of the "Catholic threat" attacking America.

# EXTRA! EXTRA!

*INDIAN SPEECH Delivered before a Gentleman Missionary, by a Chief, SAGU-YA-WHAT-HATH, which being interpreted is, KEEPER-AWAKE*

Boston Herald
September 9, 1805

A number of principal chiefs and warriors of the Six Nations of Indians, principally the Senecas, assembled this summer at Buffaloe Creek, in the State of New-York, at the particular request of a gentleman missionary (Rev. Mr. Cram) from the State of Massachusetts. The missionary being furnished with an interpreter, he spoke with them about the Gospel. When he was done, the Chief delivered the following answer:

You say you are sent to instruct us how to worship the Great Spirit, and, if we do not take hold of the religion which you white people teach, we shall be unhappy hereafter. You say that you are right and we are lost. How do we know this to be true? How shall we know

what to believe, being so often deceived by the white people?

You say there is but one way to worship and serve the Great Spirit. If there is but one religion, why do you white people differ so much about it? We also have a religion. It teaches us to be thankful for all we receive from the Great Spirit, to love each other, and to be united. We never quarrel about religion.

We do not wish to destroy your religion, or take it from you. We only want to enjoy our own.

We are told that you have been preaching to the white people in this place. These people are our neighbors. We will wait a little while and see what effect your preaching has on them. If we find it does them good, makes them honest and less disposed to cheat Indians, we will then consider again what you have said.

Now let us take each other by the hand and take our leave from one another. I hope the Great Spirit will protect you on your journey home and return you safe to your friends.

As the Indian began to approach the missionary, the missionary rose hastily from his seat and replied he could not take him by the hand, that there was no fellowship between the religion of God and the works of the devil.

Thomas Jefferson's thinking helped shape the foundation of our country. Many people assume that Jefferson and the other founding fathers were traditional Christians, but many of them were actually Deists who believed in a God that held himself separate from human affairs.

In his own way, Mark Twain (whose real name was Samuel Clemmons) had nearly as great an influence on American thinking as Thomas Jefferson did.

While a majority of American settlers held Christian beliefs, a small but influential group were freethinkers—men and women who did not follow the teaching of preachers or churches. Thomas Jefferson was a Deist. Deists like Thomas Jefferson believed that God existed but that God was not personally involved with humankind, contrary to what the Bible taught. Meanwhile, Mark Twain wrote that "Faith is believing what you know ain't so."

Although some people—like Tom Sawyer and his creator, Mark Twain—were bored with religion, more Americans were excited about spiritual matters than at any time before or since. Huge numbers of people claimed spiritual conversions, and their faith helped set the stage for nation-changing events in the following years.

# EXTRA! EXTRA!
# "MORMONS HEAD WEST"

Chicago, Illinois, Herald Press
Daily
February 4, 1846

The religionists known as Mormons (they call themselves Latter Day Saints) today left their city of Nauvoo and headed off—men women and children—to an unknown destination in the wild and unsettled West.

Our readers are no doubt familiar with the background of this famous sect, but we will nonetheless recount that. The founder of this religion was named Joseph Smith; he was exceedingly charismatic and impressed all who knew him. In 1829, Smith published a work known as The Book of Mormon, which Mormons believe is an ancient and long-lost addition to the Bible. Then, a decade ago, Smith and thousands of his followers arrived in our state and established their own city. They earned a reputation for virtuous Christian living, hard work, and cleanliness.

The reader will that recall four years ago Smith ran briefly for the office of President of our United States; and I am sure you also recall the scandal revealed at that same time. Smith announced the Mormon practice of plural marriage, and it came out that he himself was married to more than twenty "wives." This enraged the citizens of our state so much that they arrested Smith, and he died shortly after when a mob stormed the jail.

Now, Brigham Young leads the Latter Day Saints. Today, under his guidance, a vast throng of people head out of Nauvoo and toward the West, traveling in wagons, on horseback—and some on foot. Where these people will go, or what will become of them, is uncertain. They go resolutely, claiming their faith is in God.

Brigham Young

# Snapshot from the Past

## The Camp Meeting
### 1806, White Ash, South Carolina

Nine-year-old Maggie MacRae was thrilled with her first camp meeting. Workers had laid out long rows of benches, made from log planks. All the seats were filled—a whole ocean of folks was sitting there. In front of the crowd, a preacher was going at it. He carried a Bible, and he read from it some, but mostly he told emotional stories that sent waves of response through the crowd. In the front bench, repentant sinners knelt and sobbed, shouting "Mercy!" or "Lord save me!"

In just a short time at the camp meeting, Maggie had seen more excitement than she expected to get in a whole year back home. There were children all over the place. Spending a whole week camping at the meeting—this was going to be the time of her life.

# Snapshot from the Past
## The Latter Day Saints' Handcart Train Across America to Utah
### 1849, somewhere in Nebraska

Randall Robertson's feet had long ago quit hurting: now they were totally numb. With his head bent, he stared at them moving up, down, up, down.

His father walked between the two handles of the family's cart, pulling the weight of the heavy wooden contraption slowly over the bumpy trail. Randall's little sister was asleep atop the cart, lying awkwardly on the canvas sheet that

MORMONS CROSSING THE PLAINS.

covered all of the family's possessions—clothing, blankets, pots and pans, and his father's leatherworking tools, for he was a cobbler by trade. Randall's mother walked beside them, a bonnet shading her hair and face from the unrelenting sun.

For ten weeks now, they had pushed and pulled this cart: forced from their home in Illinois, to journey across endless plains, over mountain passes, across flooded rivers. A hundred carts with as many families trod ahead of them, another hundred behind.

Dreams of that land kept families like the Robertsons walking, despite their aching muscles. Sometimes they sang, to pass the time. Sometimes Mother would read from the Bible or the writings of their prophets, to encourage the family's faith. But mostly they simply trudged along, part of the long, long line of pilgrims make their way wearily toward that land where God promised they would find freedom and rest.

# Part II
# Reforming Society: 1840s–1860s

## 1838

**1838 Trail of Tears**—General Winfield Scott and 7,000 troops force Cherokees to walk from Georgia to a reservation set up for them in Oklahoma (nearly 1,000 miles). Around 4,000 Native Americans die during the journey.

## 1839

1839 The first camera is patented by Louis Daguerre.

## 1844

1844 First public telegraph line in the world is opened—between Baltimore and Washington.

## 1850

**1850 The Third Great Awakening begins.**

## 1854

1854 Kansas-Nebraska Act—States that each new state entering the country will decide for themselves whether or not to allow slavery. This goes directly against the terms agreed upon in the Missouri Compromise of 1820.

## 1859

1859 John Brown's Rebellion—John Brown leads a revolt and takes over the federal arsenal at Harper's Ferry, Virginia. However, he is soon forced to surrender by U.S. marines, and then is hung for his crimes.

**1859 Charles Darwin's "The Origin of Species," which outlines his theory of evolution, is published for the first time.**

## 1845

**1845** The potato famine begins in Ireland, driving many Irish Catholics to the United States.

## 1847

**1847** Brigham Young becomes president of the Church of Jesus Christ of Latter-day Saints.

## 1848

**1848** Seneca Falls Convention—Feminist convention held for women's suffrage and equal legal rights.

**1848(-58)** California Gold Rush—Over 300,000 people flock to California in search of gold.

## 1861

**1861(-65)** Civil War—Fought between the Union and Confederate states.

## 1862

**1862** Emancipation Proclamation—Lincoln states that all slaves in Union states are to be freed.

## 1865

**1865** Thirteenth Amendment to the United States Constitution officially abolishes slavery across the country.

**1865** President Abraham Lincoln is assassinated on April 15.

**38** *Reviving the Spirit, Reforming Society:* Religion in the 1800s

"Both North and South have been guilty before God; and the Christian church has a heavy account to answer." Harriet Beecher Stowe finished her novel Uncle Tom's Cabin, published in 1852, with these words, warning that America would suffer terribly if Christians did not

U.B. and Christian Church Miller Nebr.

end the practice of slavery. In fact, it did take a civil war to end the injustice and cruelty of slavery, but religious believers like Stowe helped create a strong antislavery movement in the years leading up to the war.

Spiritual leaders in America changed their emphasis toward the middle of the 1800s. In the early part of the century, sleepy churches needed to wake up—so preachers promoted fiery spiritual revivals. Then, in the 1830s, they changed their emphasis from revival to reform. Spiritual excitement was well and good, but thousands of "awakened" believers felt the need to do something—to make the world a better place.

Pastor Lyman Beecher in Boston and Charles Finney in Ohio led the development of the Benevolent Empire—the name given to a broad network of Evangelical Christian charities and social change efforts. The Benevolent Empire started a variety of organizations dedicated to improving society. The American Sunday School Association began in 1824 with the aim of teaching poor children basic reading and writing. Evangelical reformers built hospitals and colleges throughout the Midwest, and wealthy businessmen donated funds to run those institutions. Many of these same hospitals and schools are still open today.

The reform movement of the 1800s also sought to change laws and

**Lyman Beecher was one of the Evangelical preachers who fought to change society for the better.**

**Sunday school became an important part of American life in the 1800s, involving all ages. Often, as in this picture, Sunday school was held in the same building where the regular school classes were held during the week.**

40  *Reviving the Spirit, Reforming Society:* Religion in the 1800s

The Prohibition Party was the political outgrowth of the Evangelicals' influence on American society. This poster portrays the issues that were most important to this movement.

remove vices—practices that Evangelicals believed were harmful for society. They quickly outlawed the deadly tradition of dueling with pistols. The battle against excessive drinking took longer; the Temperance Movement against alcoholic beverages continued for an entire century, finally resulting in the prohibition of alcohol in 1920.

Most Evangelicals in the 1800s agreed on establishing charities, but they divided—sometimes bitterly—over two issues: the civil rights of women and freedom of slaves. Women held important roles in the Great Awakening and in the Benevolent Empire. However, churches and religious organizations limited women's roles: they did not allow women to speak in front of groups that included men (the Quakers were an exception to this rule). Nonetheless, women often succeeded in changing society despite these restrictions.

# Slavery: Two Views

In the 1600s and 1700s, all the American colonies bought and sold slaves kidnapped from Africa. However, by the 1800s, the development of factories in the Northern states made slaves unnecessary. Meanwhile, in the South, the cotton industry increased the demand for slave labor.

Southerners attempted to defend slavery as a "humane" institution, arguing that they helped "civilize" their African workers and provided neces-

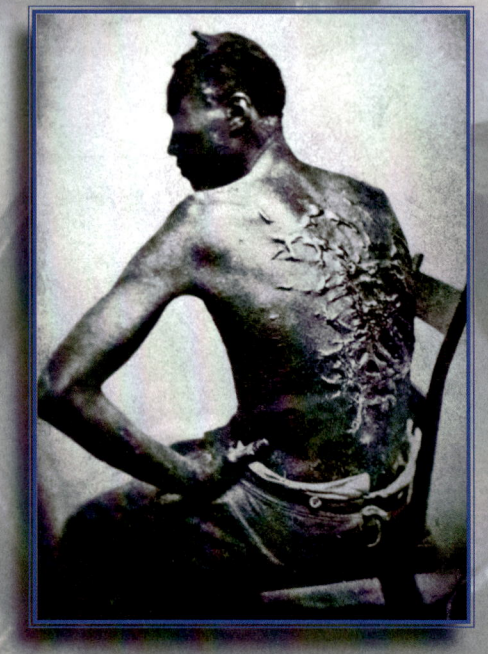

**Slavery was a cruel and terrible institution, as these pictures reveal. The drawing portrays the branding of a slave by his white master. The other image is an actual photograph that shows the scars left on a man's back after a beating by his white master.**

sary food, clothing, and shelter for these unpaid servants. However, slavery was brutal and destructive. As historian Peter Woods expresses it, "If you're a white authority, you're constantly trying to figure how . . . fierce should the punishments be? Should it be a whipping? Should it be the loss of a finger or a hand or a foot? Should it be wearing shackles perpetually?"

The Abolition Movement to end slavery began in religious circles in the 1830s. Celebrity evangelist Charles Finney preached at

# EYEWITNESS ACCOUNT

## "Ain't I a Woman?" by Sojourner Truth

Delivered 1851 at the Women's Convention in Akron, Ohio

Well, children, where there is so much racket there must be something out of kilter. I think that 'twixt the Negroes of the South and the women at the North, all talking about rights, the white men will be in a fix pretty soon. But what's all this here talking about?

That man over there says that women need to be helped into carriages, and lifted over ditches, and to have the best place everywhere. Nobody ever helps me into carriages, or over mud-puddles, or gives me any best place! And ain't I a woman? Look at me! Look at my arm! I have ploughed and planted, and gathered into barns, and no man could head me! And ain't I a woman? I could work as much and eat as much as a man —when I could get it—and bear the lash as well! And ain't I a woman? I have borne thirteen children, and seen most all sold off to slavery, and when I cried out with my mother's grief, none but Jesus heard me! And ain't I a woman?

Then that little man in black there, he says women can't have as much rights as men, 'cause Christ wasn't a woman! Where did your Christ come from? Where did your Christ come from? From God and a woman! Man had nothing to do with Him.

If the first woman God ever made was strong enough to turn the world upside down all alone, these women together ought to be able to turn it back, and get it right side up again! And now they is asking to do it, the men better let them.

Obliged to you for hearing me, and now old Sojourner ain't got nothing more to say.

his revivals that converted sinners must free their slaves and work to end slavery. Boston preacher Lyman Beecher spoke against slavery at his large church, and his daughter, Harriet Beecher Stowe, wrote her famous antislavery novel Uncle Tom's Cabin. When he met Stowe, Abraham Lincoln commented, "So you're the little lady that started this great civil war!" Quakers and other religious reformers ran the Underground Railroad—a secret network of people who took in escaped slaves, hid them in their homes and barns, and escorted them to freedom.

Christians in the South resented antislavery efforts. They depended on human bondage to keep their wealth, and they claimed God's authority to keep slaves, pointing to what they said were proslavery passages in the Bible. So in the years before the Civil War, the three largest Protestant church groups—Baptists, Presbyterians, and Methodists—split over the slavery question, with Northern churches in

## INCREDIBLE INDIVIDUAL
## Harriet Tubman

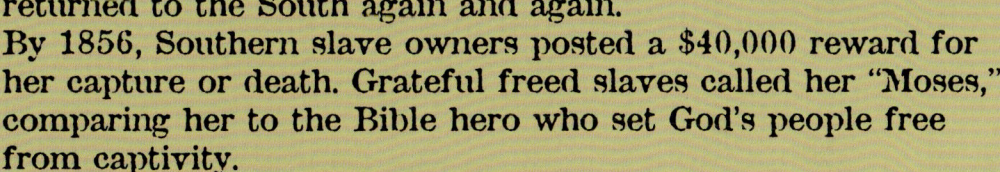

Harriet Tubman was a "conductor" on the Underground Railroad. She made nineteen trips into the South, escorted over 300 slaves to freedom, and, as she proudly claimed, she "never lost a single passenger." Tubman was born a slave in 1820. When she was a teenager, an angry foreman attacked her, and she suffered from the resulting head injuries for the rest of her life. In 1849, she ran away to freedom. She followed the North Star by night, to Pennsylvania. After that, she returned to the South again and again. By 1856, Southern slave owners posted a $40,000 reward for her capture or death. Grateful freed slaves called her "Moses," comparing her to the Bible hero who set God's people free from captivity.

all three groups favoring abolition, and Southern churches supporting slavery.

While church officials argued over slavery, the slaves themselves found secret ways to nourish their faith. Worship in most white churches meant organ playing and hymns, with the congregation sitting stiffly, but slave church gatherings were loud and enthusiastic, with "call-and-response" singing and rhythm traditions that came from Africa. White Southern ministers preached God's approval of slavery, but in their secret meetings, slaves reminded each other that God freed the Hebrews from slavery under Pharaoh—and this same God would someday free them.

*Part II:* Reforming Society: 1840s–1860s

# Westward, Ho!

While churches in the North and South debated slavery, thousands of Americans headed west. Three hundred thousand migrated to California for the Gold Rush in 1848, and masses of settlers in covered wagons headed the same way, seeking new lands to farm and make a living.

In California, religion had less influence than it did in the rest of the country. Ministers back East reminded young men heading West to stay truth to their faith, and mothers urged their sons to read their Bibles while mining. But when the 49ers arrived, there were very few churches—and vast numbers of saloons, gambling houses, and brothels. A Baptist preacher in California complained, "I have never seen a harder task than to get a man to look through a lump of gold into eternity."

**The lure of gold drew thousands of men to California. They often left the woman- and church-influenced society of the East far behind them.**

BATTLE OF CHICKAMAUGA.

# Great and Terrible Civil War

Harriet Beecher Stowe had warned that the issue of slavery might divide the nation—and it did. Four years of civil war caused the death of more than half a million soldiers, from the North and the South; but eventually, the war also freed four million African-Americans from inhuman bondage.

While young men on both sides of the battlefield suffered the horrors of cannonball and bayonet, illness, cold, and hunger, they also reached out for a comforting sense of God's presence. For the first time, chaplains served in the U.S. military (on both sides). In both camps, major revivals broke out: approximately 150,000 soldiers on each side claimed to experience religious conversion.

Weeks before the end of the war, in his second Inaugural Address, President Abraham Lincoln noted, "Both [sides] read the same Bible, and pray to the same God; and each invokes His aid against the other. . . [L]et us judge not that we be not judged. The prayers of both could not be answered; that of neither has been answered fully."

*Part II:* Reforming Society: 1840s–1860s   **47**

# Snapshot from the Past
## A Slave of Good Christian Character
## Somewhere in the South, 1849

Mr. Young had never whipped his slaves. He fed and clothed them decently, allowed time to rest in the fields, and allowed them to attend church with his family on Sundays (but seated in the slaves' balcony in back of the church). Perhaps due to these relatively humane policies, his plantation was not as profitable as neighboring farms, and he eventually went into debt. So he had to sell his slaves.

The first man on the block was an elderly man named Richard. He was frail and feeble looking, so the bidding stopped at a meager $70.00. The auctioneer, frustrated at this lack of profit, asked Mr. Young what value there was in the slave. Mr. Young replied, "He is honest and trustworthy; he attends my church and is a man of good Christian character." This recommendation of Richard's character raised his value to $200.00. He was sold, and his new master dragged Richard away from his wife, as she screamed and cried hysterically, parted in old age from her lifelong partner.

The sales proceeded until the last of Mr. Young's slaves went on auction—a teenage girl clinging to her toddler daughter. The child was torn away from its mother, and the sellers shoved the young woman onto the auction block. She begged not to be separated from her child, then fell onto her knees and prayed aloud, crying to God for mercy. This enraged the auctioneers, who flogged the young woman until blood flowed off her back and she fainted. She was hurriedly sold and dragged away.

(This is based on a true account recorded by fugitive slave Henry Bibb. He notes that this is a description of "the best side of slavery" and concludes, "The reader can . . . decide whether a man can be a Christian and hold (slaves) as property, so they may be sold at any time in market, as sheep or oxen, to pay his debts.")

# 1867

1867 United States purchases Alaska from Russia.

# 1869

1869 Transcontinental Railroad completed on May 10.

# 1870

1870 Fifteenth Amendment to the United States Constitution—Prohibits any citizen from being denied to vote based on their "race, color, or previous condition of servitude."

1870 Christmas is declared a national holiday.

# 1886

1886 The Statue of Liberty is dedicated on October 28.

# 1890

1890 Wounded Knee Massacre—Last battle in the American Indian Wars.

# 1892

1892 Ellis Island is opened to receive immigrants coming into New York.

# 1893

1893 Sri Lankan Anagarika Dharmapala speaks about his Buddhist faith at the Chicago World's Fair, marking many Americans' first exposure to Buddhist ideas.

## 1872

**1872** Restorationist Charles Taze Russell founds the Jehovah's Witnesses.

## 1876

**1876** Alexander Graham Bell invents the telephone.

## 1877

**1877** Great Railroad Strike—Often considered the country's first nationwide labor strike.

## 1878

**1878** Thomas Edison patents the phonograph on February 19.

**1878** Thomas Edison invents the light bulb on October 22.

## 1894

**1894** African American Baptists form the National Baptist Convention.

## 1896

**1896** Plessy vs. Ferguson—Supreme Court case that rules that racial segregation is legal as long as accommodations are kept equal.

**1896** Henry Ford builds his first combustion-powered vehicle, which he names the Ford Quadricycle.

## 1898

**1898** The Spanish-American War—The United States gains control of Cuba, Puerto Rico, and the Philippines.

In 1845, Ralph Waldo Emerson wrote of America as a great "melting pot" that took in people from differing cultures and races—and turned them into Americans. Others used the same term, assuming that "inferior" cultures and races like blacks, Natives, and Asians, would "melt into" American society and happily adopt the "superior" ways of white Anglo-Saxon Americans.

At the same time, thinkers and politicians coined another phrase, "Manifest Destiny." This was the belief that God intended Anglo-Americans to cover and subdue the American continent, either annihilating or "civilizing" previous occupants. They believed that God's desire for such a total conquest was both obvious ("manifest") and unstoppable ("destiny").

After the Civil War, American religious leaders continued to emphasize spiritual revival and social reform, but now they focused these energies in a new direction—the creation of a "civilized" English-culture country worshiping as educated Protestants, from sea to shining sea. Members of minorities—Irish, Hispanic, Chinese, and African-American—understandably resisted pressure to "melt" into Anglo-American identity. In the new Western states, Native peoples fought desperately against the tide of "Manifest Destiny." Because all these people struggled to preserve their identities and cultures, today America is a proudly multicultural and multireligious country.

# Back East: Revival and Reform Continue

The last part of the 1800s was an age of celebrity preachers, much like the first. However, revivalism moved out of the countryside and into the growing cities. The most famous preacher of this period was Dwight Lyman Moody, whose ministry was based in the fast-growing metropolis of Chicago, Illinois. Someone who knew Moody referred to the heavyset preacher as "two hundred and eighty pounds of flesh, every ounce of which belonged to God." During Moody's lifetime more than 100,000,000 people heard him preach, and Presidents Lincoln and Grant sat in his audiences.

**Dwight L. Moody**

At the same time, Phoebe Palmer championed social reform in the slums of New York City. Palmer was part of the new and growing Holiness Movement that emphasized clean living and charity. "Holiness is power," she declared, and she demonstrated that power by speaking in public—despite the disapproval many felt about women preaching—and by converting 25,000 people to Christian faith. Palmer believed Christians should have "tongues of fire and arms of love," and she demonstrated the latter by educating, feeding, and providing medicine to poor families in New York's notorious Five Points district. English author Charles Dickens said Five Points was "the hub of all that is loathsome, drooping and decayed," and he feared to step foot in it even with two strong policemen as guards. In contrast with Dickens, Phoebe Palmer often worked and visited in Five Points alone and unguarded.

**Five Points was a dangerous and poverty-stricken slum area in New York City during the nineteenth century.**

*Part III:* The Uneasy Melting Pot: 1860s–1890s  **53**

# The End of the Wild West

After the Civil War, settlers poured into the Western Territories, and religion soon followed, though there was still plenty of violence, gambling, and lawlessness. In the 1880s, Baptist James Spencer postmarked his letters from Butte, Montana, as sent "from Hell." Nonetheless, a growing movement of religious workers came to the West seeking to convert sinners and establish congregations.

Gunmen, saloon owners, and brothel owners used money, threats, and influence to keep preachers and churches out of their towns. To get by this, evangelists established "Sunday school" meetings in town halls and other places. These Sunday schools enabled preachers to gather congregations that eventually became full-fledged churches.

Some Wild West evangelists' preaching was very creative. Reverend Melton Jones preached in a bar in Clifton, Arizona, and compared Bible figures to the images on a deck of cards. Another preacher in Phoenix, Arizona, compared the summer heat of the town (over a hundred degrees) to the life that his sinful audience might expect in the next life—unless they heeded his message.

## Many Cultures, Many Religions

Irish immigrants continued to arrive through the 1800s, but they rarely received a warm welcome to the United States. Anglo-Americans who were themselves the children of immigrants discriminated against these newcomers, not only because they were Irish but also because they were Catholics. The Irish Catholics did not abandon their faith, however; instead, they united. Sometimes, they united to fight violence with violence, but other times they united in more peaceful ways: praying or drinking together. The Catholic Church was a vital part of their lives; Irish priests fought for their people's spiritual lives and for their human rights. Despite opposition, Irish Catholics endured and the celebration of an Irish saint—Patrick—eventually became an all-American holiday.

African-Americans, now freed from slavery, still faced violence and discrimination in the Southern states. Northern black churches sent workers to the South to minister to newly freed slaves, teaching them to read and write. In the first year after the war, the African Methodist Episcopal (AME) Church gained 50,000 members.

**Irish immigrants waiting at Ellis Island.**

*Part III:* The Uneasy Melting Pot: 1860s–1890s

By 1900, AME congregations in the south had gained 250,000 new church members. In 1894, African Americans in the south formed the National Baptist Convention, a group that today is the largest black religious organization in the United States.

Black churches after the Civil War combined the best features of two traditions: they continued the energetic preaching and worship of the hidden black churches from the past, and added organization and education gained from northern black churches. In African-American communities that struggled against poverty and racism, churches became the backbone of the community. Congregations banded together to provide food and clothing in times of shortage, education when the public schools discriminated against black children, and—perhaps the most vital thing—hope and encouragement in a hostile world. A century later, black churches would also lead the fight for civil rights.

A large African American church at the end of the nineteenth century.

In the West, Native people faced an enormous tide of settlers that broke treaty after treaty, killing off the buffalo and despising Native ways. The Plains tribes sought to find strength and comfort through the Sun Dance and, later, the Ghost Dance. The U.S. government outlawed these ceremonies and on December 29, 1890, at Wounded Knee Creek, South Dakota, troops of the U.S. 7th Calvary armed with rapid-fire guns slaughtered 146 men, women, and children of the Lakota tribe, who had gathered to perform the Ghost Dance. Other attempts to stamp out Native spirituality were more subtle: the federal government forced Native children to attend boarding schools, and the boarding school motto was "Kill the Indian to save the child." To this end, schoolteachers punished children for practicing or even mentioning their traditional dress, language, or religion. But all these efforts failed; today many Native Americans throughout the United States and Canada still follow the spiritual paths of their ancestors.

Chinese immigrants also poured into America in the nineteenth century. They worked as laborers, laying tracks for the transcontinental railroad, tunneling through mountains, and all the while, suffering from racial discrimination. While companies and bosses were eager for cheap Chinese labor, other Anglo-Americans protested the presence of this "yellow peril." Politicians spoke against the immigration of yet another "inferior" race, and even church leaders protested against the Chinese. In 1882, Congress passed the Chinese Exclusion Act, which outlawed immigration from China for the next ten years (it was then extended by the Geary Act in 1892). This was the only U.S. law that prevented immigration on the basis of race.

An image of the ghost dance was drawn on this buffalo robe. Jack Wilson, a charismatic Paiute religious leader, had a vision where he claimed God told him that if every Indian in the West danced the circle dance, they would bring the day when evil in the world would be swept away, leaving only love, faith, and harmony between the races. Whites misinterpreted the meaning of the ghost dance, however. The fact that whites saw the peaceful religious ceremony as indication that the Native people were going to rebel eventually led to the massacre at Wounded Knee.

**Chinese immigrants arrived in Oregon with the gold rush. Many worked in southwest Oregon as laundry workers, packers, and cooks. Most were single men, but a few families lived in the area.**

Anglo Americans first became aware of Buddhism through the 1893 Chicago World's Fair, where Anagarika Dharmapala, from Sri Lanka, impressed his audience with the virtues of his religion. However, Buddhists had been practicing their faith in America since 1849, when the first Chinese immigrants established their temples. As Chinese laborers moved throughout the West, building railroads and mines, they also built small "joss houses." Literally, the name meant "luck houses," but Anglo-Americans looked down on these buildings as places for "mumbo jumbo" or heathen idolatry. The joss houses were in fact Buddhist and Taoist temples, where immigrants followed spiritual traditions that were already 2,400 years old. Ironically, religion that had to be followed in secret during the 1800s is now popular, not just among Asian Americans but across racial and cultural boundaries; Buddhism is one of the fastest growing religions in America today.

# Casting a Long Shadow: Religion from the 1800s to Now

Today, fewer Americans attend religious gatherings, and more declare themselves to be "atheist" or "agnostic" than in the past. At the same time, the United States is still the most religious of the developed nations, as 80 percent of Americans say religion is "important" in their lives—a legacy of the events of the 1800s.

The revivals of the 1800s had lasting effects. Churches started in the nineteenth century—such as the Latter Day Saints, Southern Baptist, and African Methodist Episcopal—today have millions of members, and thousands of worshipers still meet in church buildings constructed in the 1800s. Preachers today still echo the teachings of Charles Finney, Joseph Smith, Phoebe Palmer, and Dwight Moody. The reforms of the 1800s are also still important, as hospitals, schools, and charitable organizations started more than a century ago still heal, educate, and feed citizens today.

A Harvard scholar recently declared the United States to be "the most religiously diverse country in the world." The presence of stupas, mosques, synagogues, and temples throughout the country demonstrates the success of people who refused to give up their religious beliefs. As a result, spirituality in the United States will continue to change; religions will develop new and surprising forms; but the influence of revivals and reforms in the 1800s will always have some impact on the ways Americans worship.

# Think About It

Religion has been a major force in American life since the beginning of our history. The 1800s saw the growth of certain trends in American religious life that continue to have a strong influence in the twenty-first century, such as a tradition of religious figures taking leadership roles in social and political movements.

- Why did people in the 1800s take their religion so seriously?

- Are people as religious today as they were in the 1800s? Why or why not?

- Religious people in the 1800s were at the forefront of the anti-slavery, women's rights, and temperance (anti-alcohol) movements. What are some of the social and political movements that are strongly influenced by religious groups in modern America?

- Does religious discussion belong in American politics?

# Words Used in This Book

*annihilating*: Destroying.
*championed*: Stood up for.
*charity*: Doing good for those in need.
*civil rights*: The freedoms that guarantee a person or groups rights of citizenship (such as voting, freedom from oppression, etc.)
*congregation*: The people who gather to worship in a church.
*conversion*: The process of changing one's life to take on the beliefs and practices of a religious faith.
*convert*: A person who has changed his or her life to take on the beliefs and practices of a religious faith.
*discrimination*: Treating some people different from others because of their race, gender, or some other characteristic.
*hostile*: Unfriendly, like an enemy.
**Industrial Revolution**: The change that took place in the world, starting about 1760 in England, when hand tools were replaced with power-driven machinery.
*inferiority*: Being lesser or not as good.
*influential*: Having power to shape people's opinions and actions.
*intolerance*: The refusal to accept differences.
*manifest*: Obvious.
*mosques*: The buildings where Muslims worship.
*notorious*: Famous in a bad way.
*previous*: Coming before something else.
*reform*: The act of changing something for the better.
*resisted*: Fought against.
*revival*: A religious awakening; a time of new religious excitement and enthusiasm.
*stupas*: Shrines where Buddhists worship.
*synagogues*: Buildings where Jews worship.

# Find Out More

## In Books

Clinton, Catherine. *Harriet Tubman: The Road to Freedom*. New York: Back Bay Books, 2005.

Horn, Geoffrey. *Sojourner Truth: Speaking Up for Freedom*. New York: Crabtree, 2009.

McNeese, Tim. *Early National America 1800–1860*. New York: Chelsea House, 2010.

## On the Internet

Mark Twain's Mississippi: Religion & Culture
dig.lib.niu.edu/twain/kastor-culture.html

Native American Religions
nationalhumanitiescenter.org/tserve/eighteen/ekeyinfo/natrel.htm

The Nineteenth Century: Divining America
nationalhumanitiescenter.org/tserve/nineteen.htm

Why Did the 1800s Explode with Missions
www.ctlibrary.com/ch/1992/issue36/3620.html

The websites listed on this page were active at the time of publication. The publisher is not responsible for websites that have changed their address or discontinued operation since the date of publication. The publisher will review and update the websites upon each reprint.

# Index

African American
    churches and communities 11, 51, 55
agnostic 60
Asbury, Francis 19
atheism 60

Beecher, Lyman 40, 44

Catholics 11, 14, 21, 24–25, 37, 55
civil rights 41, 56
Civil War 37, 39, 44, 47, 52, 54, 56

discrimination 24, 55, 57

Evangelicals 16, 40–41

Finney, Charles 10, 20, 40, 42, 59

Ireland 24, 37

Jefferson, Thomas 10, 28–29
Joseph Smith 10, 13, 30, 59

manifest destiny 52
melting pot 52
Mormons 11, 13, 30
Native Americans 14, 20–21, 24, 36, 52, 57

prohibition 41
Protestants 14, 16, 24, 44, 52

racism 56
revivals 13, 16, 18, 20, 23, 39, 44, 47, 52–53, 59

slavery 11, 13, 19–20, 22–23, 36–37, 39, 41–42, 44–48, 55
Stowe, Harriet Beecher 38, 44, 47

Truth, Sojourner 43
Tubman, Harriet 45

Underground Railroad 44–45

# Picture Credits

Archives of British Columbia 46
Creative Commons 15
J. Durham 52–53
Kasama Project 44
Library of Congress 12–13, 14–15, 16–17, 18–19, 22–23, 24–25, 26–27, 28–29, 31–33, 35, 38–39, 40–41, 42–43, 47, 49, 54, 56–58
Mexican State Government 21
Oregon State Archives 59
Our Lady of Gaudalupe, St. Louis, Missouri 21
Petr Vins 60
Wild West Show, Texas Hollywood 55

To the best knowledge of the publisher, all images not specifically credited are in the public domain. If any image has been inadvertently uncredited, please notify Harding House Publishing Service, 220 Front Street, Vestal, New York 13850, so that credit can be given in future printings.

# About the Author and the Consultant

Kenneth McIntosh is the author of more than sixty books, including titles in the Mason Crest series North American Indians Today. He also teaches college classes. He and his wife live in Flagstaff, Arizona, a town with an abundance of heritage sites from the 1800s.

John Gillis is a Rutgers University Professor of History Emeritus. A graduate of Amherst College and Stanford University, he has taught at Stanford, Princeton, University of California at Berkeley, as well as Rutgers. Gillis is well known for his work in social history, including pioneering studies of age relations, marriage, and family. The author or editor of ten books, he has also been a fellow at both St. Antony's College, Oxford, and Clare Hall, Cambridge.